MW01205917

Venom
and
Visions

Art of the Southwest

Library of Congress Cataloging-in-Publication Data

Hall, Margaret.
  Venom and visions : Art of the Southwest / by Margaret Hall.
      p. cm. -- (Shockwave)
  Includes index.
  ISBN-10: 0-531-17788-2 (lib. bdg.)
  ISBN-13: 978-0-531-17788-4 (lib. bdg.)
  ISBN-10: 0-531-15479-3 (pbk.)
  ISBN-13: 978-0-531-15479-3 (pbk.)
  1. Indians of North America--Southwest, New--Social life and
customs--Juvenile literature. 2. Indian art--Southwest, New--Juvenile
literature. 3. Southwest, New--Social life and customs--Juvenile
literature. I. Title. II. Series.

  E78.S7H23 2008
  305.897'079--dc22

2007012242

Published in 2008 by Children's Press, an imprint of Scholastic Inc.,
557 Broadway, New York, New York 10012
www.scholastic.com

SCHOLASTIC, CHILDREN'S PRESS, and associated logos are trademarks
and/or registered trademarks of Scholastic Inc.

08 09 10 11 12 13 14 15 16 17
10 9 8 7 6 5 4 3 2 1

Printed in China through Colorcraft Ltd., Hong Kong

Author: Margaret Hall
Educational Consultant: Ian Morrison
Editor: Karen Alexander
Designer: Miguel Carvajal
Photo Researchers: Jamshed Mistry and Sarah Matthewson

Illustrations by: Miguel Carvajal (pages 11, 16, and 19)

Photographs by: AgeFoto/www.stockcentral.co.nz (Spider Rock, pp. 18–19); Aurora/
IPN (cochineal insects, p. 22); C.M. Dixon/Ancient Art and Architecture (pot with bird
motif, p. 17); Courtesy of the Southwest Museum of the American Indian, Autry
National Center; 2004.29.35 (fox fetish, p. 15); Getty Images (pot with geometrical
design, p. 17; p. 23; kiva painting, p. 25; p. 30; girls in pow wow costume, p. 31);
Forest & Kim Starr (indigo plant, p. 22); Ingram Image Library (p. 29); Jennifer and Brian
Lupton (teenagers, pp. 32–33); © Michael Newman/PhotoEdit Inc. (girls in costume,
pp. 32–33); Photolibrary (cover; p. 12; group reading, p. 13; fetish bear, p. 14; p. 18;
Apache burden basket, p. 21; sand painting, p. 24; petroglyph, p. 25; silversmith, p. 26);
Tranz/Corbis (p. 3; pp. 7–10; corn design blanket, p. 13; fetish necklace and jar, p. 15;
p. 20; Navajo woman, p. 21; Navajo jewelry, p. 26; pp. 27–29; clown kachina, p. 29;
drumming p. 31)

All other illustrations and photographs © Weldon Owen Education Inc.

SHOCKWAVE
SOCIAL STUDIES

Venom and Visions

Art of the Southwest

Margaret Hall

children's press®

An imprint of Scholastic Inc.
NEW YORK • TORONTO • LONDON • AUCKLAND • SYDNEY
MEXICO CITY • NEW DELHI • HONG KONG
DANBURY, CONNECTICUT

CHECK THESE OUT!

SHOCKER

Stuff to Shock, Surprise, and Amaze You

Quick Recaps and Notable Notes

Word Stunners and Other Oddities

The Heads-Up on Expert Reading

Links to More Information

CONTENTS

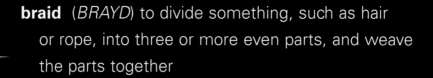

braid (*BRAYD*) to divide something, such as hair or rope, into three or more even parts, and weave the parts together

coil (*KOIL*) to wind something, such as rope, around and around

kachina (*kuh CHEE nuh*) a spirit that guides some of the tribes of the Southwest

loom a frame or machine used for weaving

mythical (*MITH i kuhl*) relating to a traditional story

venom (*VEN uhm*) a poisonous liquid produced by some snakes and spiders

vision (*VIZH uhn*) something you see that may not actually be there

weave to thread strands of fiber over and under one another

· ·

For additional vocabulary, see Glossary on page 34.

Many words can be used as both nouns and verbs. *Braid* can refer to hair that has been woven, or to the act of weaving. Other words on this page that can be both nouns and verbs are *coil*, *loom*, and *weave*.

Art is more than just something lovely to look at. It is also a way of understanding the people who created it. Many artworks started out as useful items, such as baskets. Artists added designs that had special meanings.

This book looks at the art of Native Americans of the southwestern United States and northern Mexico. These groups are known for their **weaving** and their pottery. They are skilled at making jewelry and baskets, and at painting. Their art shows a close relationship with nature. They tell stories about real and **mythical** creatures. In one dance, live snakes are part of the performance. Some of the art of the Native Americans of the Southwest is based on dreams and **visions**.

Many Native American arts are carried out today as they were thousands of years ago. The skills have been handed down from one artist to another. Arts have also changed as artists have tried out new materials or ways of doing things.

Land Settled by Native American People in the Southwestern United States and Northern Mexico

Clay sculpture of a storyteller by **Pueblo** artist Joe Cajero

For more than 15,000 years, Native American groups have made their homes in the southwestern United States and northern Mexico. In the U.S., these groups lived mainly in what are now the states of Arizona and New Mexico. The principal groups who settled in this region are:

Apache	Pueblo
Coahuiltecan	Quechan
Cocopa	Seri
Havasupai	Tarahumara
Jumano	Tehueco
Karankawa	Tepecano
Maricopa	Tepehuan
Mayo	Tohono O'odham
Mohave	Waiapai
Navajo	Yaqui
Pima	Yavapai

Myths and Memories

Southwestern Native American groups have **traditional** myths about how the world was made. The myths of each group have similarities. In many of the myths, people at first lived in a dark place. Then they came to live on the surface of the earth.

The Emergence

Long, long ago, there was no dry land. The earth was covered with water. There were no animals and no people. The gods and spirits lived inside the earth. Then the gods created living things from clay. These creatures went through changes. Some of them became people. But they still lived inside the earth.

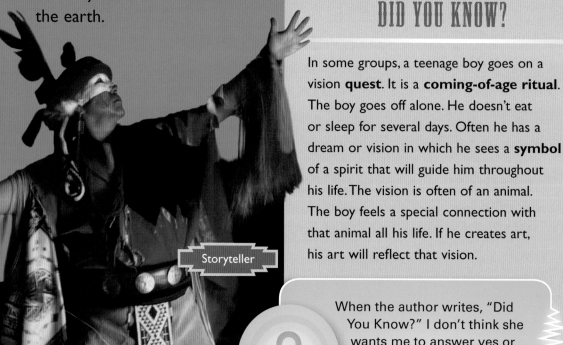

Storyteller

DID YOU KNOW?

In some groups, a teenage boy goes on a vision **quest**. It is a **coming-of-age ritual**. The boy goes off alone. He doesn't eat or sleep for several days. Often he has a dream or vision in which he sees a **symbol** of a spirit that will guide him throughout his life. The vision is often of an animal. The boy feels a special connection with that animal all his life. If he creates art, his art will reflect that vision.

When the author writes, "Did You Know?" I don't think she wants me to answer yes or no. I think it is just a way of telling me that what follows is likely to be very interesting or unusual.

The gods taught the people how to weave and make pots. The people learned the secret of fire. But then some of them began to argue and fight. The rains stopped. The crops didn't grow. Good people wanted to leave. Eventually, the chiefs led their people up, up, through all the different worlds to a hole in the earth.

After they had climbed through the hole to the outside world, the chiefs all went in different directions. Each group found a place to live. The people built homes and planted corn. They promised to live as the gods had taught them.

Storytelling

Storytelling is a very important art form for Native Americans of the Southwest. People learn about their history and traditions from stories. Many stories teach lessons or show people how to live. There are funny stories too. Some stories are about troublemakers, such as Coyote. Coyote tells lies and tricks people. Coyote is also able to tell the future.

Monsters and giants are often a part of traditional stories. There are animals that talk or use special powers. There are people who can change form. There are magical plants that help people escape from the underworld.

One Navajo myth says that Changing Woman, who represents Earth and the seasons, created human beings. She got lonely one day while she waited for her husband, the Sun, to get back, so she made humans from flakes of her skin!

> **?**
>
> This reminds me of other folktales involving animals, such as Aesop's tales, which use animals to teach us lessons about how to conduct our lives. It really helps to make this kind of connection.

Cabezon Peak

A Navajo myth says that this mountain in New Mexico is the head of a giant slain by the Twin War Gods. The twins were the sons of Changing Woman. They were heroes in Navajo myth. They made the world safe for people. They killed the monsters – such as huge birds and giants – that attacked people.

The corn plant is very important to Native Americans of the Southwest. This blanket shows corn being given to the Navajo by two sacred beings, who act as a link between the creator and the people.

Today, many traditional myths have been written down in English. People can read these stories themselves. However, storytellers still shares their tales.

Spirits in Stone

For thousands of years, Native Americans of the Southwest have carved figures called **fetishes**. Any object can be used as a fetish. However, most are small animals carved from stone. Some modern carvers use only stones found in the Southwest. Others use stones from around the world.

The **Zuni** are among the most skilled fetish makers. Zuni carvers believe that spirits live inside their carvings. One Zuni myth tells of a time when animals were turned into tiny stone figures. Later, most of the animals were brought back to life. However, some were not. Early carvers searched for stones that looked like animals. They believed these stones were animals that had not been brought back to life.

Fetishes often represent animals familiar to the carvers, such as the bear (left). Today, many fetishes are made for people to buy as works of art. To the Zuni people, the fox (right) represents loyalty and cleverness.

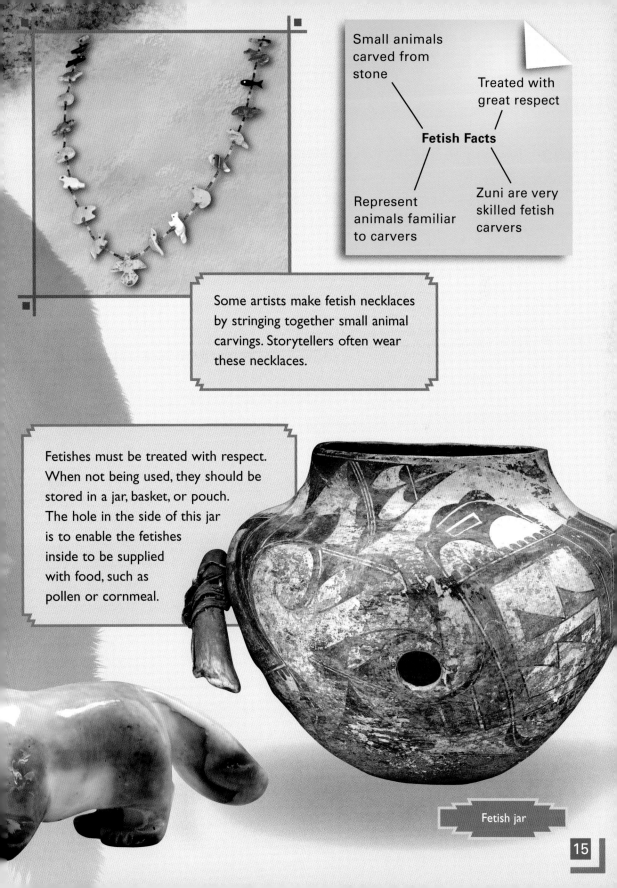

Some artists make fetish necklaces by stringing together small animal carvings. Storytellers often wear these necklaces.

Fetishes must be treated with respect. When not being used, they should be stored in a jar, basket, or pouch. The hole in the side of this jar is to enable the fetishes inside to be supplied with food, such as pollen or cornmeal.

Fetish jar

Designs in Clay

Pottery is one of the oldest art forms of Native Americans of the Southwest. Traditionally, pots and bowls were made for cooking, storage, and carrying water. Some were also used in religious **ceremonies**. Pueblo potters liked quiet while they worked. They thought that noise would cause the spirits inside the pots to break the pots.

Each group has its own distinctive designs and colors. In addition, within a group, different potters are known for their individual ways of executing the designs. Many traditional designs use shapes such as swirls and triangles. The shapes are often **abstract** forms based on natural ones. Artistic knowledge is passed down from mother to daughter.

A clay pot isn't finished until it is fired to make it hard. Long ago, potters put their pots in a fire made from goat dung. Today, some potters still fire their pots this way. Others use ovens called kilns.

Potters make their pots from clay they find nearby. The clay is formed into long ropes. The ropes are **coiled** to shape a pot or bowl. Then the surface is smoothed over.

In the past, people used jars to store water. Because the jars were not highly **glazed**, the water slowly leaked out. This leakage helped to keep the water cool.

SHOCKER

The Mimbres were a people who lived in the southwestern United States 1,000 years ago. They buried their dead under their houses with a bowl on their head. The top of the bowl had a hole in it. This may have been to let the person's spirit escape.

DID YOU KNOW?

In the past, artists used paintbrushes made from the yucca plant. They used a tool made from bone to flatten and scrape the leaves until only the fibers were left. They chewed the tip of the leaf until the fibers became very fine.

Weaving the World

The Myth of Spider Woman
A Navajo Tale

Long ago, the holy ones told Spider Woman that she had a gift. They said she could weave a map of the universe in the night sky. Spider Woman did not understand. However, one day, she went out to gather food. As she worked, she touched a small juniper tree. When she pulled her hand away, a thread went from her hand to the tree.

Spider Woman wrapped the thread around a branch. Soon she ran out of space. So she wrapped the thread around another branch. Before long, she saw that she was making a pattern. Then she knew that she had found her gift.

After this, Spider Woman started weaving at home. The holy ones told Spider Man to make a **loom** for his wife. He made a loom from Earth and the sky. He used the rays of the Sun to hold the threads apart.

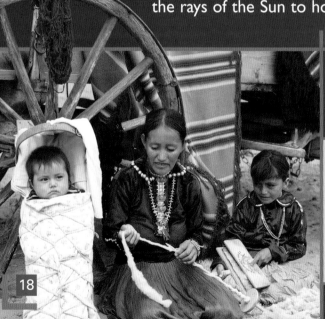

Navajo girls still learn to spin and weave from their mothers. One custom is to rub a baby girl's hands with a spider's web. This is supposed to help her become a gifted weaver.

SHOCKER

Spider Rock is an 800-foot-tall rock in Arizona. According to Navajo myth, Spider Woman lived on top. She caught bad children in her web. Then she boiled and ate them! Their bones are what makes the top of the rock a lighter color than the rest.

DID YOU KNOW?

Navajo weavers always have a thread coming out of anything they weave. It represents the line by which a spider leaves its web. This tradition is in honor of Spider Woman, who taught the Navajo how to weave.

Spider Rock

Coils and Braids

Native Americans of the Southwest have been weaving baskets for more than 10,000 years. Traditionally, weavers coated the inside of some baskets with **pitch** from trees. The pitch made the baskets waterproof. Baskets were used for gathering and storing food and water. They were used for carrying babies. They were also used for ceremonies, such as weddings. Some people buried their dead with baskets – or even in baskets.

Some southwestern groups still work in the same way as basket makers did long ago. First they collect grasses and stems of plants, such as willow and yucca. They dye the plants. Then they weave, coil, or **braid** them into baskets. Each group uses different designs. Some colors and patterns have special meanings. For example, black triangles might stand for rain clouds or mountains.

Today, many groups make baskets to sell rather than to use. However, some baskets are still made for use in ceremonies. For a **Hopi** wedding, the bride's family makes flat basket trays called plaques. These are piled high with white cornmeal and given to the groom's family after the ceremony.

Some storage baskets are so big that the weaver has to climb inside to finish making them.

A Navajo woman uses a basket as part of a ceremonial dance.

DID YOU KNOW?

Burden baskets are used for carrying things. They have straps that fasten around the wearer's forehead or back. Some burden baskets are strapped to animals.

Symbols in Southwest Native American Art

Steps: This design represents direction and change. It is used as a border pattern.

Waterbird: The waterbird symbol represents happiness. The symbol is called the thunderbird by some Native American groups.

Arrow: This is a very important symbol. It represents the life force, breathing, and the heart. It also represents protection.

Zia: This design is named after the Zia Pueblo, which used it first. It represents the sun. It also represents nature, the four seasons, and the ages of man. The symbol is on the flag of New Mexico.

Some Apache burden baskets have tin cones tied to them. The noise from the cones scares away dangerous animals.

Baskets were used for:

- gathering and storing food
- ceremonies such as weddings
- accompanying the dead

Colors on Cloth

Baskets are not the only things woven by Native American weavers of the Southwest. They also weave cloth. The earliest weavers made cloth from cotton. The cotton plant has been cultivated in Mexico for thousands of years. After the Spanish brought sheep to America, weavers started using wool.

Weavers used natural dyes to color their threads. They made their dyes from plants, minerals, and even insects. Red dye was made from the dried bodies of female **cochineal** scale insects. Blue dye was made from the leaves of the indigo plant.

Among the Navajo, it is the women who do the weaving. In the past, they wove blankets that were used as clothing by both men and women. They also wove blankets for trade. Among the Hopi, men have always been the weavers.

Cochineal scale insects live on prickly pear **cactuses**. People have been making dye from the insects for more than 700 years.

Indigo plant

Cochineal insects

SHOCKER

Natural dyes will fade if they are not treated to make them last. One way to make a color last is to mix urine with the dye. Some Native American weavers thought that children's urine worked best!

Navajo mother teaching her daughter to weave

Painting the Land

Some of the oldest pictures created by Native Americans of the Southwest were made by first chipping out bits of rock to create an image. These rock paintings are called petroglyphs. Hopi wall paintings that are 600 to 800 years old have been found on buildings used for ceremonies. When the ceremony was over, the art was covered with a layer of plaster.

For centuries, Navajo healers have made paintings from colored sand. A healer hopes that the spirits that cause sickness will be pleased by the painting. If the spirits are pleased, they will leave the sick person and enter the painting. Once the healing ceremony is over, the painting is wiped away. Today, some sand paintings are made to last. The artist covers a board with glue. Then the sand is trickled onto the board. Permanent sand paintings are not used in healing ceremonies.

Sand paintings are also called dry paintings. That's because no water is added to the sand.

Pueblo groups built brick underground rooms called kivas. Kivas were round to symbolize the pits where the ancestors of the Pueblo lived in ancient times. Kivas were used for religious ceremonies. Artists decorated the walls with paintings. The paintings often showed spirits and the essential ingredients of life, such as rain, sun, and corn. In the past, only men were allowed to go inside kivas. Today, women, too, hold ceremonies in them.

A masked lightning god and birds are painted on this 600-year-old kiva at the Kuava Pueblo in New Mexico. These symbols were used by the Pueblo people to encourage rainfall and **fertile** crops. Today, the Pueblo build their kivas above the ground.

DID YOU KNOW?

Some petroglyphs give clues to when they were made. A petroglyph that shows a man on horseback must have been made after 1540. That is when Spanish explorers brought horses to North America. A petroglyph that shows bows and arrows could be very old. Native Americans of the Southwest have been using bows and arrows for more than 1,500 years.

In the word *petroglyph*, *petro* means "rock" or "stone," and *glyph* means "drawing," "painting," or "symbolic figure." Similar words are *petroleum* and *petrified*.

Petroglyph in Utah

Blossoms and Beads

Southwestern groups have been making jewelry for a long time. Both men and women wear jewelry made of shells, animal bone, beads, and stones. Some jewelry is made of metal such as silver.

Spanish settlers showed the people of the Southwest a way to work with silver. They melted the silver. Then they hammered the cooled metal to make shapes.

Native Americans of the Southwest began to mine turquoise in about 200 B.C. Turquoise was considered to be a lucky stone. It was used to frighten away evil spirits. Turquoise often formed the centerpiece in silver jewelry. Today, the Navajo and other southwestern groups are among the world's finest silversmiths.

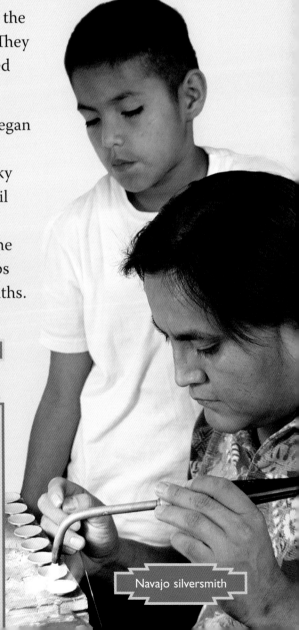

Squash blossom

The squash blossom is a Navajo design. It doesn't look like a squash blossom, though. The name may have been a mistake in translation. That often happens when words are translated from one language to another.

Navajo silversmith

Navajo silver belt buckle

Necklaces aren't the only things made by Native American silversmiths. They also make rings, bracelets, hair decorations, and belt buckles.

The word *turquoise* refers to both a color and a thing. So do the words *orange*, *gold*, and *silver*.

Traditional Apache moccasins with beadwork

DID YOU KNOW?

Early jewelry makers created beads from many things. They used turquoise, shells, wood, and bone. Apache women did especially beautiful beadwork.

Dancing With Snakes

Dance is an important part of life for most southwestern Native Americans. Many dances are a part of traditional ceremonies. Some dances are done to bring rain or to help crops grow.

The Hopi snake dance goes on for more than two weeks, in the dry summer heat. Most of the dance is done in secret. Then, on the last day, masked men dance in public. They sway, chant, and shake rattles. They do this with live rattlesnakes in their mouths! At the end of the dance, the rattlesnakes are set free. They are trusted to bring the much-needed rain.

Clown kachinas make fun of those who misbehave. In that way, they encourage people to do what is right.

Kachinas represent the ancestral spirits of the Hopi and other Pueblo groups. Each kachina represents a different spirit. Kachina dancers wear masks to show which spirit they represent. In the dances, they ask the spirits for gifts, such as rain or good health. The Hopi and Zuni carve kachina dolls from the roots of the cottonwood tree. During a special ceremony, the dolls are given to children.

Kachina dolls help Hopi children learn about their culture. Children learn what each spirit looks like, and what it does for the people.

Kachina Dolls
- Carved from tree roots
- Help children learn about their culture
- Clown kachinas encourage people to behave well

Dancers
- Snake dancers use live snakes
- Kachina dancers wear masks to identify spirit
- Ask spirits for gifts such as rain and good health

Hopi snake dancers

Cultural Connection

Traditions do not always stay the same; many change over time. Powwows are a modern way in which Native American tribes celebrate their culture. In the past, groups of Native Americans would gather to discuss matters of concern to their community. Today, powwows are usually intertribal gatherings. Non-Native Americans are also welcomed.

The gatherings are held during the summer. The strong beat of traditional drum music fills the ears. The smell of traditional food, such as fry bread, wafts through the air. Storytellers recount tales of the past.

Powwows provide an opportunity for Native Americans to wear their traditional dress, to speak their native languages, and to celebrate their myths and traditions with others.

A Navajo boy does a grass dance at a powwow. The dance has no set steps. Instead, the dancer uses the music to create a dance.

The first paragraph tells me that these pages will probably be about powwows. Being able to anticipate the contents of a page makes reading easier, and a lot more fun!

?

A powwow is a great opportunity to wear traditional dress.

Drumming is an important part of a powwow. Native Americans make musical instruments from reeds, cedar wood, sunflower stalks, and animal skins.

31

Many Native Americans keep their culture alive through storytelling and powwows. Other cultures also keep to traditions they have followed for hundreds of years. They believe it is important for their children to learn about their history, especially if there are not many of them, or they are living among people of other cultures.

WHAT DO YOU THINK?

Is it important to learn about your culture and to follow the traditions of your people?

PRO

Our culture tells us who we are and where we came from. Many traditions began for a good reason. We shouldn't stop doing these things just because we live in different times. Learning about our history and following our traditions doesn't mean we can't have fun with friends from cultures that have different traditions.

The traditions of many cultures include special rituals for teenagers. These coming-of-age ceremonies mark the transition from childhood to adulthood. The young people often have to show that they understand the traditions of their people. They need to prove that they are ready to take on the responsibilities of adulthood.

CON

Some traditions began for good reasons, but it's difficult for us to understand those reasons now. Times have changed, and it seems silly to do things just because our ancestors did them, especially if we don't know why we are doing them. I think it is more important for us to be part of the community we live in, which has its own customs.

GLOSSARY

abstract (*AB strakt*) based on an impression of something rather than an accurate depiction of it

cactus (*KAK tuhss*) a water-storing plant that is native to North and South America and usually has clusters of spines

ceremony (*SER uh moh nee*) formal actions, words, and often music, performed to mark an important occasion

cochineal (*KAH chuh neel*) a red coloring used for food and dyes. It is made from the dried female of a kind of scale insect.

Cactus

coming of age reaching the age at which you are considered to be an adult

fertile (*FUR tuhl*) able to produce healthy crops

fetish (*FETT ish*) a natural or carved object believed to bring good luck

glaze (*GLAYZ*) to paint a special liquid on pottery before it is fired in order to give it a hard, shiny finish

Hopi (*HOH pee*) a southwestern Native American tribe, part of the Pueblo people

pitch a sticky resin that is the sap of conifers

Pueblo (*PWEB loh*) the Native American groups who lived in buildings made from adobe (clay and straw). *Pueblo* comes from the Spanish word for village.

quest (*KWEST*) a search

ritual (*RICH oo uhl*) a group of actions always performed the same way, often as part of a ceremony

symbol (*SIM buhl*) a design or an item that represents something else

traditional (*truh DISH uh nuhl*) relating to a custom or belief that has been handed down from one generation to the next

Zuni (*ZOO nee*) a southwestern Native American tribe, part of the Pueblo people

FIND OUT MORE

BOOKS

Bonvillain, Nancy. *The Hopi: Indians of North America*. Chelsea House Publishers, 2005.

DeAngelis, Therese. *The Navajo: Weavers of the Southwest*. Blue Earth Books, 2004.

January, Brendan. *Native American Art and Culture*. Raintree Publishers, 2005.

Levy, Janey. *Native American Art from the Pueblos*. Rosen Publishing Group, 2003.

Morrison, Yvonne. *Stuck on Cactus: American Desert Life*. Scholastic Inc., 2008.

WEB SITES

Go to the Web sites below to learn more about the Native Americans of the Southwest.

www.peabody.harvard.edu/katsina/ceremonies.html

www.nmnh.si.edu/anthro/cm/mimbres.htm

www.indians.org/articles/southwest-indians.html

www.puebloindian.com

http://sorrel.humboldt.edu/~rwj1/navb/nov5.html

INDEX

ABOUT THE AUTHOR

Margaret Hall is the author of many fiction and nonfiction books for children. One of her favorite things to do is to take long walks, whether on the beaches of New England or away from home exploring a new place. Margaret still treasures a memento from a trip to the Southwest, a turquoise and silver necklace made by a Native American artist.